MINDFUL ME

MINDFULNESS AND DIGITAL DEVICES

BY AMBER BULLIS, MLIS

BLUE OWL
BOOKS

TIPS FOR CAREGIVERS

The rise of technology and digital devices can impact the way children interact with their peers, environment, and selves. Teaching them how to practice mindfulness can lead to positive effects on their mental and physical health. Digital mindfulness can help children be intentional with their use of digital devices and bring awareness to how screen time can make them feel.

BEFORE READING

Talk to the reader about digital devices and his or her feelings.

Discuss: What do you like about digital devices? How do they make you feel? Do you ever not like how digital devices make your mind or body feel?

AFTER READING

Talk to the reader about mindfulness and digital devices.

Discuss: What does it mean to make intentional decisions with your digital devices? How will you practice mindfulness with your digital devices?

SEL GOAL

Social and emotional learning (SEL) helps children manage emotions, learn how to feel empathy, create and achieve goals, and make good decisions. An important goal of teaching SEL skills is to provide students ways to recognize and control their emotions and behaviors. Students sometimes struggle with transitioning from digital device use to engaging in a non-digital activity. Try practicing mindfulness to help this transition go more smoothly. When students have put the digital devices away, help them pause and focus on their breathing. Allow them the opportunity to mentally prepare themselves for the next activity.

TABLE OF CONTENTS

CHAPTER 1

BEING MINDFUL

It is your bedtime. But you're winning a game on your tablet. You know you need to turn it off. But you want to keep playing. This can feel frustrating. This is a perfect time to practice **mindfulness**!

tablet

Close your eyes. Breathe in and out. **Focus** on your breathing. **Inhale** deeply through your nose. **Exhale**. Notice how your body feels. After a few minutes, open your eyes. Do you feel calm? Maybe you're ready to put down your tablet. This is mindfulness.

Digital devices are fun. But too much time on a digital device can be bad. Sitting still for too long can make your body hurt. Staring at a screen can make your mind feel foggy.

MINDFUL CHOICES

Digital devices can help us learn. It is OK to be on them if you are allowed. But make mindful choices. Be mindful of what you're doing when spending time on devices. Is it good for your mind?

Did you start playing on your tablet right after school? Pause to check on how you feel. Maybe your eyes feel sore. Your thinking feels **sluggish**. Your neck might hurt. You turn your tablet off. You decide to take your dog for a walk. Mindfulness is taking action based on what your body tells you.

GET MOVING!

Limit your screen time. What else could you do? Go outside. Get your body moving! This is healthy for your body and mind.

Mindfulness also involves paying attention. We stop to notice what is happening right now. It helps us think about our senses and **emotions**. What do you see, hear, or smell? What emotions do you feel today?

CHAPTER 2

HOW IT HELPS

Mindfulness helps us be **aware** of the present. Your grandma is over for dinner. You decide to leave your device in a different room. You want to be present.

Why should you be present?
Each time with grandma
is different and special.
You won't have this
same moment again.

Mindfulness can help you have more fun! Your friends want to play outside. It is **tempting** to watch a movie on your device. Instead, you pause. You focus on making a choice. Being with friends sounds fun. You decide you can watch your movie later.

When you are mindful, you are more in charge of your thoughts and feelings. It can hurt when someone sends a mean text message. You want to send a mean message back. But you pause first. You choose to ignore the message. You do not respond to it. Mindfulness is being **intentional** with your decisions.

CHAPTER 3

PRACTICE IT!

Father's Day is coming up. You want to make your dad a card. But you are **distracted** by your tablet. How will you make a mindful decision?

Try setting a **goal**. You can play on your tablet. But only after you have finished the card. It can be your **reward**. You finish the card. Dad loves it!

Being mindful isn't always easy. You can get distracted. Take time to pause. Think things through. How do you feel?

The next time you are on a digital device, be mindful of how much time you spend on it. Are you being present?

MINDFUL BREATHING

Try mindful breathing! Sit in a comfortable position. Rest your hands on your legs. Keep your back tall. Relax your shoulders. Focus on your breathing. Can you feel it in your belly? How does it feel?

GOALS AND TOOLS

GROW WITH GOALS

There are many ways to practice mindfulness with your digital devices.

Goal: Show your friends how to practice mindfulness! They might not understand mindfulness yet. Tell them how mindfulness makes you feel. They might like it, too.

Goal: Practice makes perfect. Being mindful becomes easier the more you try it. See if you can pause to be mindful every day for one week. Try focusing on your breathing for 30 seconds each day. Notice how it makes you feel.

Goal: Try new ways to practice mindfulness! There are lots of books to read on fun ways to be mindful. Ask your librarian for help finding one.

MINDFULNESS EXERCISE

Taking a break from digital devices can help you understand how to use them mindfully. Put away your tablet, computer, or cell phone for three days.

1. Does your body feel different without digital devices?

2. Does your mind feel different without digital devices?

3. How might you use digital devices differently in the future?

GLOSSARY

aware
Noticing and being conscious of something.

digital devices
Pieces of equipment with computers inside, such as smartphones or tablets.

distracted
To have your concentration weakened.

emotions
Feelings, such as happiness, sadness, or anger.

exhale
To breathe out.

focus
To concentrate on something.

goal
Something that you aim to do.

inhale
To breathe in.

intentional
Purposeful or deliberate.

mindfulness
A mentality achieved by focusing on the present moment and calmly recognizing and accepting your feelings, thoughts, and sensations.

reward
Something you receive in recognition of your efforts or achievements.

sluggish
Moving slowly and without energy or alertness.

tempting
Appealing strongly.

TO LEARN MORE

FACT SURFER

Finding more information is as easy as 1, 2, 3.

1. Go to www.factsurfer.com

2. Enter "**mindfulnessanddigitaldevices**" into the search box.

3. Choose your cover to see a list of websites.

INDEX

Blue Owl Books are published by Jump!, 5357 Penn Avenue South, Minneapolis, MN 55419, www.jumplibrary.com

Copyright © 2020 Jump! International copyright reserved in all countries. No part of this book may be reproduced in any form without written permission from the publisher.

Library of Congress Cataloging-in-Publication Data
Names: Bullis, Amber, author.
Title: Mindfulness and digital devices / Amber Bullis.
Description: Blue Owl Books.
Minneapolis, MN: Jump!, Inc., [2020] | Series: Mindful me
Includes index. | Audience: Ages 7–10
Identifiers: LCCN 2019021542 (print)
LCCN 2019980867 (ebook)
ISBN 9781645271635 (hardcover)
ISBN 9781645271642 (paperback)
ISBN 9781645271659 (ebook)
Subjects: LCSH: Internet and children—Juvenile literature.
Social media—Juvenile literature.
Classification: LCC HQ784.I58 B85 2020 (print)
LCC HQ784.I58 (ebook) | DDC 004.67/8083—dc23
LC record available at https://lccn.loc.gov/2019021542
LC ebook record available at https://lccn.loc.gov/2019980867

Editor: Jenna Trnka
Designer: Molly Ballanger

Photo Credits: shapecharge/iStock, cover; hocus-focus/iStock, 1; sirikorn thamniyom/Shutterstock, 3; thechatat/Shutterstock, 4; Shyamalamuralinath/Shutterstock, 6–7; VaLiza/Shutterstock, 8–9; Wave Break Media Ltd/Dreamstime, 10–11; aldomurillo/iStock, 12, 13; gradyreese/iStock, 14–15; Syda Productions/Shutterstock, 16–17; Monkey Business Images/Shutterstock, 18, 19; Angelafoto/Getty, 20–21.

Printed in the United States of America at Corporate Graphics in North Mankato, Minnesota.